Network and Multi-Level Marketing Mastery:

Follow The Ultimate MLM Business Guide For Gaining Success Today Using Social Media! Learn The Pro's Secrets on Attaining More Sales, Using Facebook, and More!

Graham Fisher

Table of Contents

Introduction

Hello and welcome to network and multi-level marketing mastery!

In this book, we are going to learn about the amazing results you can achieve with your own multi-level marketing/networking business. Many people view multi-level marketing with a suspicious eye, thinking that it's nothing more than a pyramid scheme. While some unethical pyramid schemes try to pass themselves off as multi-level marketing firms, the reality is that a legitimate multi-level marketing company is not a pyramid scheme. Real multi-level marketing businesses are legitimate, selling legitimate products to real customers, and are not simply about endless recruiting of members.

Topics that we will cover in this book include:

- Learn the difference between network marketing and multi-level marketing (MLM).
- Get insight into the proper mindset for starting an MLM or network marketing business.
- Tips and tricks on finding the right company.
- Building your own brand.
- Planning and executing events.
- How to present your opportunity to prospects.

- Your two income streams: distributors and customers.
- Utilizing social media for your MLM/Networking business.
- Building your downline.
- Handling rejection.
- Top reasons people fail to make money.

Time can't be wasted, so let's get started learning about getting into the MLM and Networking business!

Chapter 1: What you need to know about network and Multilevel Marketing

Let's face it – the general public doesn't have a positive perception of multilevel marketing. Their views have been colored by a few bad actors. These are people who've run pyramid schemes that appear to be legitimate MLM businesses but really aren't. Those kinds of companies rely on an endless recruiting chain, which is they only keep operating by recruiting new sales associates without actually moving product to the buying public. These types of companies are viewed with suspicion and seen by the public as "cheesy" and rightfully so.

What is it that distinguishes them from a real MLM business? If you could distill that down to one concept, it would be this: a legit MLM business has two revenue streams. One is in fact recruiting new members to build your downline (downline are sales associates you recruit, you get a cut of their sales, upline are people above you who get a cut of your sales), but a real MLM company also sells a legitimate, useful product to the public. That second piece forms an important part of each member's sales income.

In fact, a legitimate MLM business isn't really all that different from any other type of business; it simply uses different methods to recruit sales staff and get the product in front of paying customers. In the latter case, it's about getting customers personally and directly involved with the product so they can see it and sample it before buying.

Historically many very successful businesses that have grown into giant companies were built this way. One of the most famous is the California Perfume Company, which was founded way back in 1886 by a man named David McConnel (funny but true – the company was based in New York despite its name).

The company had more than a hundred perfume products that were sold across the country, using a staff of tens of thousands of direct sales associates. In 1937 the company changed its name to Avon. It's still going strong, with net sales surpassing $100 million a year. Today, Avon has more than 6.4 million sales representatives. Avon operates in more than 100 countries and uses a direct sales model, which includes multi-level marketing.

The undisputed king of multi-level marketing is Amway. Founded in 1959, the company sells a wide array of home products including household cleaners and health and beauty products. The company's sales routinely top $8 billion annually.

Knowing how to spot a pyramid scheme

Amway was investigated by the Federal Trade Commission (FTC) in the late 1970s for being a pyramid scheme. The FTC found that Amway was not a pyramid scheme, and the case is instructive for anyone who wants to get involved in multi-level or network marketing, so that you can recognize if any company you are thinking of joining is a pyramid scheme.

The business model in a pyramid scheme is based on paying people to recruit others to the business. Generally, a business based on a pyramid scheme will require a payment to join the business. Then it will promise payments to sales associates for recruiting new members to the operation. The upline gets a share of the payments, so the directors of the company typically enjoy high, passive incomes. One thing often missing from such schemes is a legitimate product with value to sell to the public.

When pyramid schemes to involve a product, they often require members to buy large quantities of the products which turn out to be very hard if not impossible to sell. Pyramid schemes also don't require members to have retail sales; instead, they focus solely on recruiting new members to the scheme.

In a real MLM company, while upline members get payments from sales made by the downline, they are not getting *paid to recruit new people*.

The FTC decided that Amway was not a pyramid scheme. Among the reasons given were:

- Amway does not pay distributors to recruit new members.
- Amway requires distributors to maintain a minimum level of retail sales.
- Amway does not require distributors to purchase large stocks of inventory.
- Members must accept returns of excess inventory from downline sellers.

The main things to keep in mind are whether or not the company requires you to pay to join, if you will get paid to recruit others, and most of all whether or not the company has a legitimate product that sells. If a company strikes out on all three of these items, it's a good idea to look elsewhere.

What is the difference between multi-level marketing and network marketing?

Generally speaking multi-level marketing and network marketing are the same thing. However, there are some specifics related to "network marketing", which is often focused on product events. Event marketing is a method that sales associates can use to get in personal touch with prospective customers and let them try out the products in face-to-face interactions. There are many different ways this can be accomplished. The sales associate uses event planning for a wide variety of events that allow people to try out the product and potentially join the business themselves. A live sampling of products can occur at parties, "trade shows," conferences, or even online in webinars, which are large online group meetings. Social media provides many new opportunities for network marketing as well.

As such, you can see that network marketing is really an extension of traditional multi-level marketing or a different technique. While Avon has traditionally relied on door-to-door sales, a modern network marketer may use an online webinar or host an event to drive sales and recruit new members.

Often many people use the terms network marketing and multi-level marketing interchangeably.

Should you build your own business from scratch or start network marketing?

In today's economy, there are more ways to start your own business than ever before. It's easier than ever to start from scratch, but it's no piece of cake either. Despite the increased accessibility people have to products and markets, starting from scratch is going to be very hard work. And of course that isn't to say that multi-level/network marketing with an existing company is easy or automatic either, but in that case, a lot of the groundwork has been done for you.

Starting your own business these days will often involve some type of internet presence. One very popular method being used today is opening a Shopify store. Alternatively, you can start selling products on Amazon in its marketplace, or even go the hardest route which is to design your own website from scratch.

The online approach can save you some hassle because you can base your business on drop shipping. In other words, you can have companies shipping product for you behind the scenes without having to keep inventory.

Another popular approach is to brand products that are manufactured in China and other countries. For example you can use Alibaba to find products made in China that you can brand or customize to sell as your own products. This process can be entirely automated once you get it set up, with the shippers sending products to a network of distributors in the United States and other countries that can ship them to customers for you, or ship them to large marketplaces like Amazon who will hold them in storage until orders are processed.

You can even design your own products and have manufacturers overseas build and ship them for you.

This is quite different from networking and multi-level marketing for the most part, however, as you will probably not be having direct contact with customers. You could set up your own sales staff built on a multi-level marketing model with it, however, but you'd have to set up arrangements to get the product to your sales staff. Opportunities do exist for using webinars and other online "events" with your own products as well.

The biggest downside that you will encounter starting from scratch is your products will be untested in the marketplace. They may succeed – and that is great if they do! However many people wishing to get into business would prefer to market a tested, proven product with a well-known brand. Of course, a great way to do that is through multi-level marketing.

Consider a fictitious woman named Lisa James. Lisa goes all out the hard way, and finds several health and beauty products on Alibaba. She has them branded with the Lisa James brand after hiring a designer to make a logo, and waits several weeks for samples to be sent from China. After she approves the samples, she waits several more weeks for a large shipment of product, and then she launches her Shopify store and begins selling Lisa James cosmetics.

Customers have never heard of Lisa James before so they will have a natural barrier to simply buying the products.

Her friend Marsha, on the other hand, decides to become an Avon representative. After some training, Marsha is able to go out and begin selling Avon products. Many customers are easy sales since they are very familiar with the brand name which is instantly recognizable worldwide. Marsha mixes it up, setting up a website to sell Avon products and also doing in-person product demos and events, including recruiting some new members. While Marsha keeps some product on hand, she doesn't need to keep much since Avon can take care of everything on that end.

These two examples are not to say that one method is better than the other rather that they are different paths each with their own strengths and weaknesses. Which path you choose will depend on your own personal preferences. If you would prefer to sell a product that is already established and well known, and take advantage of being able to be involved in live events, direct sales, and recruiting downline members who can increase your income, then multi-level or network marketing is probably what you are looking for.

Keep in mind that these two approaches are not necessarily mutually exclusive, but starting from scratch to build a network marketing business is going to be a lot more work and success is far less than guaranteed.

With multi-level/network marketing, you also know that while nothing is guaranteed, it's based on a system that is proven to work. Amway has been selling well since 1959 – think about that.

In the digital world, there is also an alternative known as affiliate marketing. As an affiliate, you can sell other people's products online and receive a commission for your sales. Methods used for affiliate marketing include running ads on digital platforms such as Facebook, setting up websites and blogs to promote the product, and using email newsletters to sell products. You can promote affiliate products for major operations like Amazon.com or sell individual products found on commission websites like clickbank.com and jvzoo.

Benefits of network marketing companies

Let's summarize the benefits of going with an established network or multi-level marketing company.

- Startup costs are low. In fact compared to most businesses they are vanishingly small.
- You gain instant brand recognition (examples Avon, Amway, Mary Kay cosmetics).
- You can develop a passive income stream if you build an effective downline.
- If you work hard, you can quickly build a full-time income. With that comes personal freedom. You can work when you want and how much you want.
- You could do sales working for a company, but you're an employee if you do so. With network marketing, you're your own boss to a large extent – but as someone who owns their own business, you get tax benefits an employee cannot get for their activities.
- Support – the people above you provide a great support structure that can help you learn the ropes and get the most out of your business. If you start from scratch, you have nobody there to help you.
- Training and branding. Again, starting from scratch, you're on your own. When you join a network marketing company, you'll get training that will help you grow and excel.

Chapter 2: Mastering Your Mindset

Regardless of which path you take, mastering your mindset is important above all else. An attitude of success is vitally important, and people often don't realize how they are sabotaging their outcomes with pre-programmed mindsets. These mindsets can be subconscious programs that lead to a mindset of poverty and failure. You don't have to be starving to be in a poverty mindset, the subconscious programs may be merely keeping you from reaching your potential, or maybe you find yourself living paycheck to paycheck barely able to pay the bills. A poverty mindset may impact the way you relate to co-workers and sales prospects, making your presentations fall flat. It's important to have an attitude of plenty and success before striking out on your own.

Envision your dreamy end goal

The first step in mastering your mindset is to know where you are going! The answer to this question is different for everyone, so it doesn't have to be lounging on a beach in Tahiti, although that will certainly count! Your end goal might simply be having an extra $2,000 a month. It might be making a solid six-figure income, or you may be aiming for becoming a seven-figure seller who attains wealth beyond your wildest dreams.

The end goal is adjustable, so you don't have to set an end goal now and be satisfied with that for all time. However, it's very important to have a fixed end goal so that you know where you are going. Not knowing where people are going is one of the premier mistakes made by new business owners.

Spend 10 minutes a day daydreaming

It's important to condition yourself into accepting that the end goal is possible, that the results you envision are real, and that they are within reach. You need to condition your subconscious mind to accept this as a reality. One way to do this is through repetition. Begin by taking ten minutes of each day to daydream about your end goal. See yourself living that goal, no matter how big or how small your end goal is. Something else to consider is that the subconscious operates more in the domain of dreams and feelings than it does in logic. So don't say to yourself "I'm going to make an extra $2,000 a month", see yourself how you'd be living with that kind of change in your life and *feel* it instead. How would it feel to have all your bills paid each month? Experience the results – you'd be more relaxed and confident. This mentality will start to actually sink in and you'll begin living the end result making it more likely to materialize.

And remember to dream big – as big as you want to! People routinely achieve seven-figure incomes in networking and multi-level marketing, and you can do it too. So if your goal is to take it on full-time and take things to their limit, then daydream about earning riches and living in the type of lifestyle you dream about, including travel, nice homes, and being able to give back financially to others.

List 3 things you want to achieve

It's one thing to dream, but the next step is to set specific goals and achieve them in real life. Begin by looking at where you are now and what the end goal is, and then start breaking down what you need to do in order to reach the end goal in concrete steps. The steps should be broken down in such a fashion that reaching intermediate goals is relatively simple, especially at first. For example, if you are totally brand new to multi-level marketing, your first goal could be to check out five multi-level marketing companies and do research on each company, learning what products they sell, what their payment structure is, what kind of training and support they offer, and how much you can make from recruiting others.

The near-term goals should also include specific outcomes that take you closer to your ultimate goal in concrete steps. They should also include deadlines. For example, you should make a goal to be active with one of the multi-level marketing companies within 2 weeks. The time frame is only for the purposes of illustration, but you should not choose a time frame longer than that because one problem people have with striking out on their own is putting things off. In fact, most people procrastinate when it comes to launching their own business to the point where it never gets done. So you need to be proactive about getting things done in short time frames to ensure you don't end up being one of those people who will start a multi-level marketing business "one of these days".

The power of three is a great way to set goals. Start off by setting three concrete goals you know you can achieve in the next 14 days, and keep them in a journal or logbook where you can track your progress.

Give yourself a pep talk

It seems silly to many people, but giving yourself a pep talk to keep your head up is important, especially in the beginning when you're going to face obstacles, make mistakes, and possibly see some failures. The best salespeople are always upbeat and optimistic, and it is important to keep yourself in that frame of mind no matter what types of problems come up. You can include some affirmations in your pep talk. Remember to say them repeatedly so that they move into your subconscious mind and become emotional states that in turn act outwardly improving your results. Some examples:

- I feel the wealth that is going to be part of my life.
- I am a champion!
- I approach people in a warm, friendly, and likable way.
- I have a prosperity mindset.
- I want to build success and share it with others.
- I am trustworthy and will provide support to my networking team.
- I can learn anything and will master any training I need to be a successful network marketer.
- I care about other people.
- I sell products that make other people's lives better.
- I will share my wealth and help make other people wealthy.

- I will attract prospects who are dedicated to helping others as much as they are dedicated to building their own wealth.
- I am happy and dedicate myself to the service of others.

The last affirmation is especially important. SERVICE TO OTHERS is one of the most important mindsets you can adapt for any business, and that is true for network and multi-level marketing as well. The more you dedicate to service for others, the more you will be personally rewarded as well, not only in financial wealth but with a network of supportive people who know you are someone they can count on and trust. When it comes to building wealth, you are paid in proportion to the amount of service that you provide others. Maximize the amount of service you offer and your income will increase.

These affirmations are only suggestions, you can create many of your own that you think will help you reach your goals. Say them at least five times per day. Repetition is vitally important when it comes to making something part of your subconscious.

Hold yourself accountable

While pep talks, dreaming, and affirmations are all important, without real action in the real world, we get nowhere. That's why it's important to hold yourself accountable. If you set goals and don't achieve them within a specified time frame, then what is the point?

Begin by writing a personal mission statement – this is your dreamy end goal. Again, it can be as big or as small as needed to fit your personal situation and where you want to go.

Then, list the 3 things you want to achieve in writing. These should then be broken down into sub-goals that are easy to achieve. List specific time frames to achieve each sub-goal. Sub-goals can even be broken down into daily to-do lists, the more you break things down the more you ensure that you are taking steps toward the end goal.

At the end of each week, review your performance. Which sub-goals for the week were not met, or were met in unsatisfactory fashion? Identify them and note the reasons why you failed.

Holding yourself accountable means really making things right. Therefore, you need to take action to respond to a goal that wasn't met. Here is an example – suppose that someone gave you a certain amount of money to budget for a business goal, but you totally blew it. Is standing up and saying "I take responsibility for this" holding yourself accountable, or is doing that *and* cutting a check to pay the money back holding yourself accountable? It's the latter.

When you hold yourself accountable, there need to be real-world consequences for doing so.

Pay attention to your thoughts

Remember we are all a collection of microprograms in our subconscious minds, many of which were put there starting at birth. It can be difficult to undo the negative programs that govern our lives while we aren't even really aware of it. Most of us go through our day with thoughts that arise from these micro-programs without really paying attention to them. Start by paying attention to your thoughts and become consciously aware of any negative thoughts you are having that may keep you from meeting your goals. Then take action by replacing those thoughts with positive thoughts that will help you meet your goals instead.

Stay curious

The most successful people in life are those that remain curious. People often think of curiosity as a characteristic of children, but in fact, it's a characteristic of leaders. The world is constantly changing and lifelong learners are going to be the ones who attain the most success. Curiosity also cuts across all aspects of life, a successful multi-level marketer is curious about the needs of their prospects and their associates and is eager to learn.

Chapter 3: Choosing the Right Company for You

If you're just starting out, choosing the right company is going to be one of the most important steps you take as a budding network marketer. It's going to be an important decision that can make or break your first year in the business. Of course, it's not the end of the world if you start off with the wrong choice, but any time wasted is a huge setback when it comes to reaching your goals. So it's better to put the homework ahead of time so that you choose the right company.

People often ask if you can work for more than one multi-level marketing company. Technically speaking, the answer is yes you can. However, that is probably not the best decision. One thing you need to avoid in business is being wishy-washy, and when you're not 100% dedicated toward something, wishy-washy is exactly where you are going to end up. That isn't to say that you can't make money going with more than one multi-level marketing company, but it's probably not the best course of action.

Think about some of the things that can determine success or failure. Three items come to mind:

- Commitment.

- Passion and enthusiasm.
- Deep knowledge of what you're selling.

Don't you agree that being successful in selling products and recruiting others to sell those products is going to require all three? You're not going to be getting the most success when you're a "jack of all trades" in this industry. It's far better to know a narrow product line extremely well than it is trying to learn and focus on multiple product lines from different companies. Again, we are not saying that's impossible, but most people are not going to be up to it – especially beginners.

Think of famous athletes that played multiple professional sports. Yes, a few are successful, but the vast majority don't get near the success they would have by becoming a complete master of one sport. The athlete who dedicates their entire existence and training too football is going to be a better football player (all else being equal) than the athlete that spends half the year playing baseball.

Choose your niche and discover companies

With that in mind, it's important to select a niche that you are passionate about. If you have a REAL passion about a niche, it's going to flow out of you naturally leading to more success selling a product in the niche and recruiting others. Imagine just picking something just because it makes money and then being stiff, boring, and coming across as "fake" when trying to sell it. It won't work!

Before even looking at companies, get a notebook and start writing down things you are interested in that might be sold by multi-level marketing companies. It could be skin products, cosmetics, or diet aids/vitamins. It could be vacuum cleaners. It doesn't matter, just write down a list of at least five difference niches that you might be interested in. The best niche you can choose is going to be one that you are passionate about.

Passion is important. Of course, if you are passionate about something, but nobody is selling it anywhere, then that passion isn't worth a dime. There has to be a balance between your passions and what is actually offered by various networking businesses. One of your first steps is going to be matching these up.

Then examine each niche further. Begin by looking at a niche and finding out what companies are available, if any, for a given niche. Begin listing them along with important information regarding each company. For example, you'll want to note:

- What is the pay structure offered by the company?

- What products are offered that match up with my chosen niche?
- How reasonable are the products? Are they legit? Are they priced at reasonable prices so that people are not being exploited?
- Will you feel good about yourself selling these products?
- What training programs are offered by the company?
- What is the company asking of new people that join?
- Do you feel that the company offers adequate support?

Write down the answers to all these questions for each company that you look at. Then you can use the results to begin to whittle down toward a company you decide to join.

Remember, that while we emphasize doing your homework ahead of time, choosing a company is not a life or death decision. If you join a company and feel like it is not a good fit, simply drop it and move on to a different company. Your long-term success requires that you have a good fit with the type of company, products, and the company itself.

Stability and longevity of the company

You should consider the stability and longevity of the company. It's possible to jump on board with something new and achieve the heights of success, but one way to make success far more likely is to go with a system that is proven. Think of the most commonly known examples of multi-level marketing companies – Amway, Avon, Mary Kay Cosmetics, etc.

Why are these companies so well known? One reason is they offer high-quality products, and they have a system that flat out works. Remember Avon has been around since 1896! They must be doing something right.

You can't go wrong by going with something that is proven to work. That doesn't mean you have to go with the oldest company around, but you should consider the history of the company. If you find a company that has only been around for a year, it might fail. It may be that the product is a fad product and not sustainable over the long-term. Some companies end up in legal trouble for various reasons, maybe they are selling a bad product that could harm consumers, or they are a veiled pyramid scheme that isn't the best fit for sincere people who want to do network marketing as a legitimate business.

So, longevity is clearly in the companies favor. If a company has been around a long time, we know that:

- It's selling products that the buying public wants.
- It's not primarily based on short-term fads. The company probably adds new products to its line, but it probably has a secure base that works in evergreen fashion.
- The company treats members well; it won't survive if people are not able to become successful multi-level marketers.
- It's not getting into constant legal trouble.
- Simply put – it has a proven system that works to move product and make for successful multi-level marketers.

Also, look at the earnings of the company. Are they growing, or at least stable? A long-term company can be a sinking ship. So make sure that even if the company has demonstrated longevity that it's still pulling in respectable revenues that are not declining.

Stability fits in with these points listed here. As we said with Amway, it had even been investigated by the FTC for being a pyramid scheme, but they found out that was not the case. Amway has been around for more than fifty years, making it a solid bet – it's legal, it sells products people want, and with more than $8 billion in sales, it's making money.

But keep in mind that longevity isn't everything. If you used longevity as your only criterion, you might be stuck with IBM and have missed Facebook, Amazon, and Google. Quite often, new companies burst on the scene that offers high-quality products that they can use to establish themselves in a solid niche. It's important that you go with something you're passionate about over simple stability. If you are bored with Amway's products, you're not going to be a good fit for them.

While Amway and Avon have been around a long time, you might look at companies that are relatively new but have been in operation for more than a decade, so show some stability. One company that fits that profile is NHT Global, which offers a wide variety of products that can be sold via e-commerce with annual revenues of around $1.5 billion.

Evaluate the products and services

Before jumping on board, you will want to actually check out and use the products and services offered by the company. If you're going to be effective at selling something, you'll want to know that product inside and out. Suppose that a company was selling a keto diet meal plan, home delivered. Do you think you'll be more successful selling that product to others if you've actually eaten some of the meals? What if they taste lousy, or are too hard to make? You will look shallow and foolish if you are trying to sell something you really aren't familiar with.

Also, you'll want to evaluate the products and services offered by these companies so that you're more likely to choose a winner. If you can actually experience the product and see that it's high quality, then you'll have more confidence in going with that company because you'll know it will be easier for you to make sales and have happy customers. You may also find subtle differences between different products and services, helping you weed out similar companies to find one that is most suitable for your goals.

Learn about the compensation plan

When you begin doing research on MLM companies, the compensation plan is going to be one of the most important considerations. Note that they are sometimes referred to as "comp plans." So you'll have to learn about the types of compensation that are offered.

First a couple of definitions:

- Downline: These are members that you've recruited to the organization. Their sales and referrals will also generate income for you.

- Upline: The person who recruited you to the company. Also, anyone in their upline is in your upline.
- Distributor: Someone who sells products for an MLM company.
- Personal Volume: Usually the volume of retail purchases by your customers, but can include your purchases as well.
- Commission: The percentage paid to a distributor for closing a sale. Often, this is calculated as a percentage of the dollar amount of the sale; however, sometimes, it is calculated based on personal volume.
- Frontlines are the distributors that you recruit. So think of the frontline as your personal sales team, with you at the top (of course you are below someone in the upline who recruited you, and they have their own frontline). Your frontline distributors, if they stay with the company, will develop their own frontline by recruiting members.

Unilevel organizations

Unilevel organizations have a simple structure that is probably closest to what you think of when conceptualizing network or multi-level marketing companies. In a unilevel organization, anyone you recruit becomes one of your frontline associates.

Commissions are paid up several levels deep starting with the lowest frontline associate that make the sale. Companies restrict how many levels deep commissions are paid, about five levels is typical. Members of a unilevel organization may be able to supplement income with paid bonuses. Pool bonuses can be used to pay members who are top-level distributors, while a "fast start bonus" can help compensate new sales associates who are otherwise receiving small commissions.

In order to start earning money and succeed in a unilevel organization, you're probably going to have to recruit a large number of new distributors. This can be a disadvantage because most people are not that great at or interested in recruiting new members. If you have to recruit a lot of new members to the organization, you'll be devoting less time to sales and more time to training and managing new members.

One advantage to a unilevel organization is that you will see a faster rate of income generation than you would with other types of organization. Everyone in a unilevel organization gets paid the same bonuses despite rank.

Differential bonus

With a differential bonus, commissions from a sale are divided into portions. The higher you are up the chain, the more portions you qualify for, but if people in the downline are there and they qualify, they get to take their cut first. The portions you are qualified for depend on your rank. To make it simple suppose people are ranked rank 1, rank 2, etc. So let's see how a differential bonus could work in an organization. As a salesperson gains more experience (and we assume produces results), they gain more rank.

Imagine that a $100 sale is divided into six portions. The newest distributor who is rank 1 gets one portion, or $16.67. If there is a rank two distributor above him, she gets two portions, or $33.33, but less the portion of the distributor below her. So she also gets $16.67. The rank 3 distributor qualifies for three portions, but only gets all three if there is nobody downline. If there are rank 1 and rank 2 distributors below her, she also gets one $16.67 portion from the sale. However, if there are no rank 1 and rank 2 distributors, then she would get all three portions, or about $50.

Breakaway

In a breakaway compensation plan, the basic unit is a group with a leader at the top. If you achieve "breakaway rank", you can leave the group and become the sales leader of your own group/sales team. In a breakaway system, the group leader is entitled to all portions of a differential bonus, but the portions taken by people downline are subtracted. So continuing with the previous example, if there were rank 1, rank2, and rank 3 people downline, they would each take their slices of the commission at $16.67. That would leave half of the commission left for the leader, so they take all 3 remaining slices or about $50. If you are the leader of a breakaway group and qualify for the entire bonus, then you've effectively cut off the upline from qualifying for any bonus.

Level bonus

In the plan described above, you may qualify for three portions of the commission if you are rank 3 say, but if there are people of lower rank in the downline then you only actually get a smaller portion. A level bonus works differently; in that case, you get the commission payment you are entitled to receive regardless of the people below you. In other words, if you are entitled to 33% of the commission, you'll receive that even if a rank 1 person below you gets their 16.7% commission.

Binary

This type of organization is structured differently than a unilevel organization. Binary organizations only allow each distributor to have two frontline distributors. These form two "legs". If they recruit more, those people are placed downline, in a process known as spillover. This type of organization is good for new members, as they can get recruits placed under them from spillover. The distributor will receive a 10% commission on the "weak" or pay leg, which will be the leg that would generate a smaller volume of sales. One advantage of binary compensation plans, is they limit the number of people a distributor has to recruit. In fact, it is typical to find that distributors recruit 2-3 members anyway, which fits in well with a binary compensation plan but may not fit well with a matrix (see below), depending on how it is structured. Binary organizations have more direct support for new recruits, helping them become productive members of the organization. Unlike in a unilevel organization, in a binary you're going to have a strictly limited number of distributors to manage and train. In a binary structure, like with unilevel, there are ranks but people are all paid the same bonuses.

Matrix

If the organization has a matrix structure, then distributors are grouped according to a fixed width and depth. So as an example, if it was a 3 x 3 matrix, there could be three distributors directly below you, and including yourself the matrix would be 3 levels deep. So you would get paid to 3 levels down in the organization and each member below you would have 3 distributors, just like you do. If the matrix was 3 x 5, then you'd have 3 distributors immediately below you, and you'd get paid 5 levels down. You can only recruit a fixed number of distributors, so any further recruits will be placed below your other distributors using spillover. Experts in the industry consider narrow and deep matrix arrangements to be better than shallow and wide arrangements because deep and narrow increases the support beneath you. So a 2 x 10 matrix would be better than a 4 x 3 matrix. A wider matrix will require more effort to recruit the necessary number of associates to fill the matrix.

Know your company's plan

Before choosing a network or multi-level marketing company, it is important to know the compensation plan that the company uses. You should take into account how much time you want to spend recruiting new members, training and so forth.

If that is not something that is up your alley, you may be more interested in a binary plan.

Pay attention to the team you are joining AND the team you will build

When you join a network marketing organization, you'll begin by joining an existing team, and then you'll be building a team of your own as you begin to grow your own business. High commission rates are good, but you'll also want to be comfortable with your team.

- Are these people you are comfortable spending time with?
- Do they seem honest and sincere?
- How do their goals align with your goals?
- Do they share your same values?

Evaluating the team you are joining is as important as evaluating the products and services the company offers. If the team is not a good fit, you aren't going to be happy and may not do well as a result. When you need training and mentorship, if you don't feel comfortable with the team members, you may avoid getting all the help you need. Instead, look for a team you gel with, and your success is more likely. If you can't get along with the team at the first company you look at, consider finding a new one instead.

When recruiting your own team members, you'll want to consider the type of person that you want to recruit. For example, are you going to prefer educated team members? While a college degree may not be a requirement, you may find that requiring more education can help you filter out inappropriate team members. You're also going to need to know their life goals. Are their life goals consistent with yours? Obviously, you want team members that have consistent goals so that you're all working toward one end.

What's great about today's world is that while the old methods of building MLM teams are still around, it's also possible to leverage technology to recruit team members. You can start by having your own website and collecting email addresses of people interested in joining. Write a blog about your network marketing venture to drive traffic to the website. You can also leverage Facebook and Twitter to find new members, and you might be able to employ digital advertising. One advantage going to the web has in getting your network marketing business off the ground is that you won't have to plead with friends and/or family members to join you on your MLM adventure.

Determine if the business fits your goals

Aligning with the team is important, and so is aligning with the company. In order to maximize your success, you're going to want to seek out a business that fits your goals. First and foremost determine whether or not the company will help you achieve the financial goals that you've set out to achieve. Remember that you can't take shortcuts in life, and if you've set high goals, then you need to find a company that can deliver those results if you put in the hard work. You are not going to want to be joining up with a company that will limit your financial and personal growth.

You're also going to want to look at the values of the company as well. Do you believe in the company's mission and the products or services they offer? Do they share your views on the environment, health, and religion? If not, then you might be better off looking for a different company. There is no shortage of good MLM companies these days so don't think you have to get on board with the very first one that you find.

Making the final pick

To summarize, you're going to want to learn:

- When was the company founded and how long has it been in business. Has it been embroiled in any controversy or even legal trouble? If so, how did those situations work out?

- Educate yourself on the team members at the top! Learn who they are and what their backgrounds are. Are the members in the c-suite well-suited to the long-term success of the company? Are they outsiders or did they work their way up?
- Evaluate the company's products or services. You should obtain samples, buying them if necessary. The best way to know the company is by using their products. Do you want to attach your name and personal reputation to a second rate product?
- Know the company's compensation plan and study its advantages and disadvantages.
- Determine how much time you'll have to spend training, and mentoring and team building. While network marketing derives profits from the sales activities of new members you recruit, if too much effort must be devoted to activities related to recruitment, how much time is left over for sales? Remember that ultimately you have to sell actual products.
- Examine the ability of the company to help you reach your ultimate financial goals.

- Determine if the business aligns with your values.
- Do the products the company offers align with your passions? Remember to choose a niche you are interested in so you can maximize success.

Remember, the world is full of network marketing companies – you don't have to settle. At the same time, you don't want to keep pushing goals forever to the future by not picking one and going with it. When you're just getting started, you should probably move forward with a company and see how it works out for a few months. If it isn't to your liking for one reason or another in the future, there is no rule that says you have to stick to that company for life. Value the fact that you're more experienced with network marketing, and find a new company that is a better fit.

Chapter 4: Making a Commitment to Growth

People who are involved in networking or multi-level marketing are an optimistic bunch. And with good reason – they are pursuing a life of financial freedom and personal liberty. These are two results that are possible when entering the world of network marketing and getting the success that you seek.

Sales also play a central role in this type of lifestyle, after all its network *marketing* and multi-level *marketing*. As you are aware, you cannot succeed in sales without optimism, a commitment to teamwork, and a growth-oriented mindset

Learn to see the good in things

Life in the world of network marketing not only involves sales. You're going to have to recruit new members, and as a small business owner, you're going to have to be able to bounce back quickly from setbacks. People who see the good in things are more able to do all three with success.

Whether you're selling a product or recruiting new members, you're going to be more likely to close the deal if you're an upbeat and positive person. Part of that will stem from seeing the good in things. Seeing the good in things begins with seeing the good in others, and that begins with seeing the good in yourself!

People are their own worst self-critics. Often this goes to excess as people beat themselves up over minor setbacks. To be clear, we are not saying you should not be accountable for your actions or that you should just brush off mistakes. Quite the contrary – you must be accountable for your actions, and you need to learn from your mistakes. Otherwise, you cannot move forward and grow.

However, learning from your mistakes doesn't mean beating yourself up over them. Everyone makes mistakes. Learn from them, and take action to correct for them. If you've done something really bad, then atone for it to make it right. In either case, you shouldn't dwell on any negativity. You pick yourself up and move on.

When thinking about yourself, separate the mistake or bad deed from you as a person. An act and a person who commits the act are not one and the same. You are not determined or defined by your mistakes. Think about yourself in a positive light by using daily affirmations.

Seeing the good in others may require you to confront your own biases, and recognize that you are too critical or judgmental. However, it's an exercise worth pursuing since studies show that seeing the good in others leads people to greater happiness. And when you're happy you're optimistic, and it will make it easier to sell more products and recruit more members to your MLM organization!

Oftentimes, it's not worth the negative energy to go around criticizing others. If you have a negative outlook and look to be judgmental, people are not going to like being around you. Certainly, people that you are trying to sell to or recruit are not going to enjoy being around an old curmudgeon who is critical and resentful. Being critical of others does nothing but create negative energy, and makes it harder to succeed in other aspects of life.

The same results from events you encounter. Remember, that you are what you think. If you have a poverty mindset, you will attract poverty into your life. If you begin interpreting events in a negative way, then they will always have a negative impact on your life.

Who do you think will be a more successful network marketer? Sally, who is bubbly and optimistic, and is looking forward to earning an extra $3,000 a month, or Joe, who says "I hate MLM companies, but I can't find a job doing anything else!" Obviously, Sally is more likely than Joe to succeed, although we can hold out hope that Joe will gain a more positive attitude once he starts training and making sales.

However, most of the time, people who think like Joe and who view things in a negative light don't succeed. *You are what you think* is a good motto to keep in mind.

You can also help yourself become a better salesperson, mentor, and recruiter by developing a more friendly and outgoing demeanor. Smile at people more and be sure to make eye contact. Shake their hands with a firm handshake. When someone is talking to you, spend more time listening and less time directing the conversation. Make them feel like the conversation is about them. Project a warm and friendly demeanor.

Another piece of advice is to stop being so cynical. These days we are awash in negativity. Don't impugn others intentions and see them in a positive light until proven otherwise. Look for the positive in people and events.

It's often hard to see at the time, but even the most catastrophic events in your life will have some positive glimmer in there somewhere. Learn to look for it and seek it out.

The bottom line is that if you are an optimistic person, seeing the good in others and in things, you're going to be more successful. Negative energy translates into failure and creates conflict. So why give into it? Instead, take the opposite path which is more likely to lead you to the road to success.

Commit to working hard toward success

One thing is for sure; nobody builds a business without putting in hard work. It can't be said enough: there are no get rich quick schemes. Learn to accept that and accept the reality that success and meeting your goals is going to require hard work. That doesn't mean you have to kill yourself; in fact, you may not even have to work full-time in multi-level marketing to make a success out of it. That said, you should always set realizable goals that can help you establish and grow your business, with at least one goal accomplished per day. If you are unable to work full-time on the business, each little goal you accomplish daily is a baby step forward, and those steps add up over time.

Unfortunately, we're surrounded by a lot of information about the business. We're told that you can constantly travel and live on your laptop, running your business from anywhere. That isn't to say there isn't some truth to that, but you should have a realistic picture of what it means to be in business. You are definitely going to have to put your time and effort in. You can work smarter rather than longer; the number of hours put in certainly isn't the only metric. However to get things done and be successful both time and effort are going to be required.

Continue approaching growth with consistency and passion

Passion is a key ingredient in the success of any business. It's especially true in multi-level marketing. Without passion, you have nothing. If you have passion, your own passion can be enough to move mountains. Or more importantly, close deals!

Respect yourself and your needs

You should always respect yourself. That can mean not letting the business destroy you, your personal life, or your family. Remember that ultimately life is all about balance. If you are making great money but working so much that you never spend time at home with the children or walking the dog, then you are doing too much at work. Keep things in balance for long-term success, and that means limiting time spent working or thinking about working to a certain number of hours per day. It also means taking time out for yourself each day, and that can include time spent with the family in the evenings and engaging in activities like walking the dog. You should also listen to your body's signals, and recognize times when you're going to need rest. Getting sick or developing a major illness is never worth closing another sale.

Focus on expanding in every way that you can

The sales associate who keeps growing is the one who is more likely to move up the ranks. You need to keep learning and focus on expanding in every way. Continually make lists of your shortcomings and come up with plans to fix them. For example, if you're nervous about public speaking or aren't quite sure how to go about doing it, consider enrolling in Toastmasters. If you're not up to speed on the technology used in your industry, find online resources to help you learn about it. You don't have to go back to school and get a full-time college degree, look for courses on Udemy that can help you improve your knowledge.

Someone once said that if you're not growing, you're dying. This saying is so true, especially if you work in the network marketing industry. It's a competitive world out there, and it's constantly changing. Those who push themselves to grow are going to be more successful than their competitors. Customers will take notice – they instinctively know who the growth-oriented people are and they will tend to follow those folks.

As an individual sales associate, you're not all that different from a civilization or nation-state in some ways. Anyone who has studied history knows that a civilization that reaches out, explores, innovates, and leaves itself open to new ideas is one that will grow and possibly take over others. On the other hand, civilizations that turn inward tend to wither up and die. A good example is Europe in the 15th and 16th centuries; it had an outward focus based on growth – and grow it did for many centuries. On the other hand, China at the time decided to turn itself back. It sought the safety of staying within its own lands and gave up growth. At the time, both cultures were at about the same technological level. A couple of centuries later, Europe had far surpassed China on almost every front.

If you're the kind of distributor who is always growing, whether its learning new products, new sales techniques, or the latest online technologies and methods that can help you grow your business, you will far surpass your competitors who are stagnant.

Be willing to seek and accept feedback from others

None of us can go it alone. While Albert Einstein managed to do so, the vast majority of us aren't that clever. We need feedback from others in order to improve. When you join network marketing or MLM organization, you should begin seeing yourself as a team member, and not just as someone who has an independent sales business. If you're a beginner, in most cases things are not going to run perfectly smoothly right out of the gate. You should seek the assistance of people with more experience in the business who are willing to mentor you. Being around great teachers is a great way to get started.

Second, you're going to be making mistakes, and often, people are going to see the mistakes you make. You should be open to constructive criticism, rather than getting defensive or reacting in knee-jerk fashion. In many cases, people will want to help you. They all want the company to succeed, and often because of the way these companies are structured your success means the success of the upline. So they are not your enemies they are on the same team and have a personal stake in your success. So you shouldn't ignore any feedback offered by other team members. Take it to heart, analyze it, and make a logical and detached judgment to the extent possible as to how you'll accept the feedback and use it for self-improvement.

Commit to learning about your business and industry

When you join a network marketing or MLM team, it's very important to join a company that has products in a niche that you are interested in. To be successful, you're going to have to know the business and industry inside and out. You're going to have to know the products inside and out. If you don't, how on earth are you going to convince other people that the products are good to use? If you don't really know the products, people will quickly see through that. If you don't really know about and believe in the company, people will see through that as well.

On the other hand, if you know every detail the way you'd expect a surgeon to know your anatomy and come across as a confident expert, people will believe in you. And people who believe in you are going to be people who trust you and will buy from you if they are customers. If you are trying to recruit new members, people who believe in you and trust you are going to be anxious to join your team since this will help them to believe in the possibilities of success and achieving their own goals.

You shouldn't just know the individual products you're selling and the company, you need to be familiar with the industry at large. It's also going to be important to keep up on a regular basis so that you know market trends and where the industry is going. You'll need to be up to speed on the main competitors to your company. That includes not only knowing their product line and its quality but also knowing what the company is researching and what its own growth plans are. You can't do this for every single business in the world, but there are probably 2-3 leading competitors in your industry. Focus on them and know them as well as you know your own company.

Learning about the business and industry will take time and effort. But it will pay off ten-fold later. You're also going to need to realize that this is not a one-time endeavor. The markets are constantly changing, and that will probably be true of your market as well. As a result, you can't be asleep at the wheel; you're going to find that competitors will be making new adjustments and introducing new products all the time. Your own company will be doing the same. It's going to be important to keep up.

Chapter 5: Promoting Your Products and Events

To succeed at networking and multi-level marketing you need to sell! Selling involves selling your products – and also involves selling your opportunity to prospects who may be good candidates to join up as distributors. In this chapter, however, we will focus on selling products.

The idea of having to market and sell products can intimidate a lot of people. This can be especially true of new people joining a company that sells using an MLM system. The reason many people get intimidated is that the process often involves in-person interactions where sales prospects are invited to actually try the products. Many new people aren't confident that they can sell in person, but if that describes you don't get discouraged. It's actually not as difficult as it might seem at first.

Before we proceed, we'll note something important. We've been saying that you should find a product, niche, and business that you are passionate about. When you begin to contemplate the idea of selling the products in person, then it comes home why it's better to be passionate about your niche. The person who is excited about what they are selling is going to come across as sincere and have no problem highlighting the benefits of a given product. Those who are simply doing it to make extra money and don't really care about the product will come across as fake and cheesy. It will be even worse if you are not enthusiastic at all, your presentations will come up flat and fail to attract buyers.

Luckily we live in an era when the internet and smartphones have massively expanded opportunities to find and sell prospects. You can leverage Facebook and other social media to help build your brand and schedule events. You can even use webinars to demonstrate products to a worldwide audience (provided you've set up a way for them to order of course). You can even leverage Craigslist, to set up meetings/events and promote them for free, provided you're a little bit careful about it.

Build a brand for yourself

The first step in creating a brand for yourself is determining what you want to brand. There are two general options, but they aren't mutually exclusive. The first is to brand based on the product. That doesn't necessarily mean you should zoom in to focus on one specific product; your branding should be on the niche the product is in which can offer you some flexibility.

However when branding remember that part of branding is going to be positioning yourself as an expert. The more narrow the niche, the more credible the expertise is going to be. People are going to be skeptical if you try and position yourself in multiple ways; in other words, you won't seem as credible if you try to be an expert on skin products and in auto repair. Even if you are a "renaissance" person who really can fix their own car, that just doesn't look credible at all to most people, and the two areas should be kept completely separate. But that doesn't mean you're totally limited either. Establishing yourself in one niche will open doors for related niches. So if you positioned yourself as a health and fitness expert, easing your way into nutrition is a natural fit.

So, there are two major options when it comes to branding. One is to brand your business, and the second is to brand based on the product. Branding your business is going to include branding based on network/MLM marketing itself. That doesn't mean that you're not also going to be promoting products, but you'll lead with talking about making money, the lifestyle of being a business owner (personal freedom, travel, be your own boss, etc.), working with your sales team, how to set up a network marketing business, and so on. A large part of business branding is going to be leveraging your niche to recruit new team members.

On the other hand, if you lead with the product, then you're going to spend most of your time promoting the specific niche that you've chosen and the products related to that niche. That means spending a lot of time discussing the types of problems that are solved with your products and talking about the products themselves.

Again, this is not really an all or nothing proposition; it's a question of what you *lead with* and what your primary focus is on. If you lead with product branding, you're going to be putting most of your effort into promoting the product and talking about that niche, but that doesn't exclude you from some level of business branding – obviously, you are going to be doing both. If you do product branding, then your efforts at including business branding will be a side venture. If you are using a website to promote your business, then you will have one page on the site devoted to recruiting new team members, by promoting the idea of "hey, if you are passionate about x and would love to earn money promoting it, contact me."

If you decide to brand on a product, this can be done on multiple levels since few products really operate in isolation. Consider that you may decide to sell multiple health and beauty products. You could sell skin care products but also be selling diet pills. One way to increase your income is to sell multiple products to the same clients, and you may have noticed that lots of women that buy skin care products are also going to be interested in buying products related to weight loss and fitness. Not all of them will, but a significant fraction most certainly will be interested. So if you have access to products from all three niches, then you're probably going to want to brand yourself focused more on a generalized niche, as opposed to only being an expert on skin care products.

But there is no one-size-fits-all answer when it comes to making this decision. You are going to have to evaluate where you're at in your own personal situation, what company you work for, and what products they have available. You can brand a product line rather than branding a business if it's more appropriate for your situation. Ultimately the question of how your brand is going to be based on what you enjoy doing the most.

In other words, the key factor that should always be taken into consideration is passion and excitement. If you are super-excited about a product, then you could be better off branding based on the product. Remember that when you're doing promotion, you're going to have to spend a lot of time thinking about what you're promoting, possibly writing about it, whether on Facebook or on a blog and selling online and maybe in person as well. So you'd better be enthusiastic! The key concept is to set up your branding in the best way that is in synergy with your passions. You may be equally passionate about skin care products and weight loss products – in that case, you should brand your business and promote both. But if weight loss products don't excite you to nearly the same degree, then you should brand based on the skin care products.

On the other hand, if you are most passionate about having your own networking business (as opposed to specific products to promote), then you'll probably want to devote more time talking about and promoting that.

Regardless of which path you choose, part of the branding process is positioning yourself as an expert. When you are just getting started, a more limited approach to branding that is product-based is a better approach, because it's easier to position yourself as an expert in one specific area as compared to trying to be a jack of all trades. Also, a newbie to network or multi-level marketing will be less credible talking about the MLM lifestyle than they will be talking about a product or niche.

Branding can evolve with time just like anything else. So you can start with a complete focus on skin care products, and after you're well-established with that begin to incorporate weight loss products into your business and branding.

However, building a *personal* brand is probably the best ticket to success over the long term. A personal brand isn't tied to one specific product, network marketing company, or even niche. We'll hope that you don't jump around between network marketing companies unless it's absolutely necessary since you would lose a lot in the process (flushing your team), but the point is a personal brand is tied to YOU as the expert. The specific skin care product, to choose an example, will be far less important if you've correctly positioned yourself as an expert. If people perceive you in this way, then no matter what kind of skin care products you recommend and sell, people are going to buy in based on the reputation that you've started. A personal brand can be tied with products or leading with a business.

Establishing yourself as an expert begins with education. So you need to learn as much about your niche as you can. If you plan to brand leading with network marketing and lifestyle, then you need to learn all you can about that. But no matter what you do, there are going to be specific things you need to get in place to do your branding efforts.

- Get a logo made. This doesn't have to cost a lot of money, find someone on Fiverr to make your logo. Decide beforehand if you want a personal logo to represent you like a personality (think Martha Stewart or Tony Robbins), or do you want a logo to represent a product line in the niche? Be sure to check out previous designs made by the prospective hire and read their reviews before spending any money.
- Create a website for your niche. Even if you are going to be focused on marketing locally, you should have a website. It's practically expected these days. If you are selling physical products, Shopify is an excellent choice. But if you use Shopify, you should have your own domain to make it look professional, rather than telling the world you're an amateur just starting out.
- Create a blog, and post about your niche daily. At first, the blog isn't going to do much for you, but over time your blog will begin attracting large numbers of people. The specific issues related to building a blog are

beyond the scope of this book, but you should learn SEO and utilize Google Keyword Planner and other tools to ensure that your blog brings people in. If you do decide to opt for a Shopify site, you can build your blog right into the site.

- Create a YouTube channel. If you aren't comfortable speaking on camera, start practicing. A YouTube channel is one of the most effective ways to get a free promotion that there is. Not having one should be a criminal offense – yes it's that good. Also if you decide to do advertising, you can post videos and use them to advertise on other YouTube channels and videos at very low cost. You can use YouTube videos to demonstrate products, and then link back from the video to your Shopify (or other) store, and you can connect your blog as well.

- Create a Facebook Page. Once you've set up a blog and YouTube channel, the Facebook page is a snap. You provide content on the Facebook Page by linking back to your blog and YouTube channel. The backlinks will help your blog rise in the search engines as well. If you decide to do Facebook advertising (something that should always be a consideration in any business), you will need a Facebook Page.

- Get Business Cards printed with your logo on them, and your links to all your online channels and with your email address. Yes, the old-fashioned methods are still important, especially if you're considering doing local events.

- Consider signing up with ClickFunnels. This is an easy to use tool that lets you set up "landing pages" online. Simply put, this is a single web page that is designed to get people to sign up with their email address, so it is used to collect leads. You should set up landing pages for your product business and also recruit new team members. Later you can promote them using YouTube or Facebook ads.

Take advantage of video marketing

As we've said above, YouTube is one of the most effective ways to promote your business. This can be done for free, by simply putting together a solid YouTube channel, and at low cost by using your videos to create ads that run on YouTube. The same videos can also be used in Facebook ads. You can also expand your reach by posting videos on other platforms like Vimeo.

Video marketing can take place on multiple levels. Start your channel by introducing yourself, what you're niche is and so forth, within the context of your branding decision. If you are leading with the business, then you may want to make a video talking about network marketing and use it for recruitment of new team members.

Product demonstration videos will be an extremely important part of your business. Remember to link the videos back to your main website and your blog, where people can purchase the products. You should also link to landing pages, as having an email list is one of the most important tools a marketer can use online. Once you have an established email list, you can email people with new products and special offers, and watch the revenues pour in.

Video marketing can also be used to help set up online or local events. Online, you can create what is called a webinar to discuss a product live in front of an online audience. Webinars often lead to massive sales. You can also utilize these to recruit new team members, selling your "opportunity."

Create content specifically for your ideal client

In any business, you need to know who your primary customer is. Not their name or personal identification, we are talking about knowing what the most likely type of person is to buy your product. You will want to know their age range, gender, what they are most likely to do for a living, and what their interests are. This information can be used in multiple ways. For instance, you can use it to laser target prospects on Facebook. You can also use it to set up marketing videos. For example, if you find out your main prospects are 45-60-year-old women, if you are not a female in that age range, you can recruit someone to help you make a product video. When your main prospects find the video on YouTube, they will subconsciously see themselves in the video and see the benefits of the product more clearly.

One way that you can find out who your ideal customer is will be by using Facebook ads. You can run small Facebook ads without targeting any specific demo, and then build up data on who responds to the ad – this will tell you who the ideal client is. Once you have that information, then you can laser target on all platforms.

This approach works whether we are talking about marketing a product or service, or for finding prospective team members.

Attend events that your audience would attend

Besides knowing who your average client is, you should put yourself in their experience set. Attending events that your audience would attend will help you do this. You can also spy on the competition to help yourself up to your own game.

Show products in use

Whether you're making a video, at a live in-person event, or doing a webinar, showing the products in actual use is going to be one of your most effective marketing tools. At live in-person events, people will be able to sample products for themselves, but you can also garner huge benefits by doing demonstrations on video.

Don't focus entirely on sales

The most effective marketing technique that there is can be described as follows. You don't sell products; you establish a relationship with your clients. This is one reason that personal branding is important. The central focus of building a relationship with your clients is to build trust. This can be done with in-person meetings but can also be done very effectively by using email marketing, blogging, YouTube videos, and your Facebook page. Don't make every post about selling a product – in fact, you should make a minority of your posts about actual selling. Spend most of your time talking about your niche and provide useful information. Then prospects will begin seeing you as a trusted expert in the given niche – and when you do recommend a product, they will be eager to buy because they trust your recommendations.

Chapter 6: Presenting Your Opportunity to Prospects

The difference between a network and multi-level marketing business is that your business exists on two related but independent frames. On the one hand, you're selling your products, just like any other retail business or sales operation. But in the case of network or multi-level marketing, you're also selling your *opportunity*. That is, you're recruiting people also to become sales associates themselves. This helps the company out by getting more people pushing their products, and it helps you since you'll get a commission from the proceeds of your downline (the people you recruit to join). The bottom line is that a bigger team/downline means a larger commission check – so it is really important for the growth of your business.

Of course, this aspect of the business is what gives it a negative connotation among some members of the public. They see MLM and network marketing folks as pushy and even cheesy. But you can avoid this perception by approaching your recruiting efforts with care. Simply put, don't be pushy about it. And although there is no doubt you're probably excited (and maybe a little obsessed) with your new lifestyle and earning an income for yourself, you don't want to come across as being completely focused on it. Remember our approach to promoting products? We said don't always focus on sales – build trust instead. The same advice applies here.

Last but not least don't over promote to friends and family members. No business opportunity is worth alienating your friends and family. Instead, you can recruit them via ACTION and RESULTS. If people see that you're becoming successful, making more money, and living a lifestyle that includes more personal liberty and financial independence, the results will speak for themselves. That by itself will attract people to your opportunity.

Another great source of prospects for the opportunity are your own customers. But again, you don't want to be pushy about it, but at the same time let them know that the opportunity is there if they want it. Many of your customers will be as passionate about your products and niche as you are, and so they will be intrigued when they find that they too can make a living promoting it. The key is to go about doing it the right way so that you don't push them away.

Invite them to approach you

Leveraging the power of being able to recruit team members to your network marketing business is what helps drive dramatic growth. You're not going to grow nearly as much as you really can if you're only focused on selling products, you want to build a team who is working with you to sell more product and expand the team even further leading to even more growth. This is the true power of network marketing.

The first rule of success is to avoid being pushy – and you can do that by inviting prospects to approach you, rather than going out and hard selling them. This can be done in multiple ways and via multiple venues, both in person and online.

Let's begin by simply focusing on your interpersonal relationships. If you are excited about your product and your new network marketing business, then the first thing to do is carry that enthusiasm over to your personal demeanor. You want to be the outgoing, friendly person who always has a smile on their face. Happiness and optimism are contagious. People are drawn to others who are enthusiastic and happy. But of course, you don't want to overdo it – be enthusiastic without being a nut. You want to make people feel comfortable around you.

Second, successful network marketers are always making new friends. The more friends you make, the more opportunity there is to recruit new team members. By simply being friendly, along with being optimistic and enthusiastic, you're going to invite others to approach you about opportunities. Be sure to get out there and attend events related to your niche so you can constantly make new friends who share this interest. Being an expert in the niche helps to – if you are the one person who seems to know all the important details, people will be drawn towards you and begin viewing you as an authority figure.

Part of making new friends and drawing them in is being a storyteller. People love storytellers, and if you can weave stories together that also involve your niche and your business, people will become interested in the business.

Inviting people to approach you doesn't have to be something that you only do in person – you can do it online as well. You can make short videos talking about your opportunity and post them on YouTube and on your Facebook page. This should be done within the context of promoting the niche itself so that people view it as an "aside" rather than your main focus. It's the same as promoting the product; you want 80% talking about the niche and only 20% talking about the product. That's even more important here; you don't want people having their stereotypes confirmed, that is thinking that network marketers are obsessives that belong to some kind of cult. Invite people to approach you subtly, and you'll have success.

Let them ask the questions

One of the most important things to do when selling is showing people how a product or service solves some problem that they have. When you are recruiting, you're not doing anything different; you're still selling. So what problems do recruiting someone to a multi-level marketing business solve? There can be many reasons that a person might become an interested prospect:

- Their job doesn't pay enough, and they are having trouble making ends meet.
- They have a huge debt and need a second stream of income to help pay it off.
- They can't stand working in an office and want to start a home business.
- Tired of the 9-to-5, they simply want personal liberty in their work life.
- Financial freedom is a long term goal, and they're looking for an opportunity to make money that goes well beyond the income you get from a regular job.
- Many reasons only they can tell you...

An effective approach to recruiting someone is to show them how joining your team is going to solve their problems. So you have to find out what their problems are. When you find out what is currently causing pain in their life and what their long term goals are, then you can show them how joining the network marketing business will solve their pain problems and help them reach their goals.

You can't just jump in and do this. You need to begin by establishing trust with the prospect. Building a rapport with them is what is going to lead them toward a place where they're able to reveal this information to you. You don't want to be high-pressure or come across as the aggressive salesman. Establish a relationship with people and then let them ask questions about your business.

When they start opening up to you about the pain points in their life, you can use that as an opening to talk about your business. You can explain how the network marketing business solves their particular problem. If they are looking to make extra money, talk about how your position helped you earn an extra $3,294 when you first started the business. If they want flexibility, talk about how you work when you want and where you want. When bringing up pain points, let the prospect lead you where they want to go, but then you offer the solution.

Remember to tailor your pitch to each individual that you engage with – there is rarely going to be a one-size-fits-all solution to everyone's problems.

Finally, you will want to create a unique selling proposition. What makes your network marketing company better? Why should the prospect join your team, as opposed to joining some other network marketing company? Make sure that you know what your unique selling proposition is and how to communicate that to your prospects effectively.

Lead the conversation without pressure

Putting pressure on a prospect will do one thing – push them away. Never make your conversations with people salesy in nature. Make them seamless and genuine.

Subtly create a sense of urgency

A sense of urgency is one of the oldest sales tricks in the book. When someone has an interest in an opportunity but is sitting on the fence, they will suddenly become more interested if they find out that the opportunity is expiring in 48 hours or 7 days. This technique is used by all kinds of businesses; for example, a grocery store will get more people inside the store by offering time-limited coupons. Once inside the store, people will end up buying lots of other things too, which far outweighs the discount they got on the coupon. Car lots will sell at a discount "this weekend only." A sense of urgency gets people to take action – because the last thing they want is a lost opportunity.

You never want to put pressure, but you'll need to let people know that the opportunity is only available for a short time, or that it's far better to act now rather than later. For example, you can say "we will be finalizing our team next month," or some other time-limited excuse. Again, don't be high pressure about it, and never make it act now or else – but let them know that if they don't join soon, they will be losing the opportunity.

Have a resource available for them to read over

Always be prepared. You never know when prospects are warm to jumping on board, so you need to have materials at your fingertips to hand out when someone expresses interest. Otherwise, you'll lose the opportunity.

Always request to follow up

Many people aren't going to sign up the very first time you talk to them. You'll need to warm them up a little more to get them on board. We just discussed one way to get that done – be prepared with resources for them to read on their own. Then you're going to want to follow up. Never leave a conversation without getting an email address or phone number (or better yet – both). An email address will allow you to share more resources, such as your YouTube videos (another reason you should be making them). You can share information about the products you sell and call to discuss things with the prospect. Many people will simply need some reassurance before they make the commitment, and being able to do it with a phone call or video will help them get over the hump.

When considering follow up, remember that you should never be a pest or an annoyance. High-pressure tactics simply turn people off rather than getting them to join their team. A good thing to do is to create a short email follow-up list of prewritten emails that describe the business and how it can work to create income, wealth, and freedom for people. When you meet new prospects, you can add them to the email list and let it do the selling. Start with a "Thank You" email.

You can call about halfway through and say "hey, just wondering if you happened to read my email about..." Use the emails to continue building more trust as you simultaneously warm them up to saying yes to the offer. Follow up calls can be used to answer questions that the prospect may have, and for you to overcome their objections. Also, provide more than one avenue to get in touch with questions. Some people may not want to discuss this over the phone or in person; they may find it high pressure. So you can relieve the pressure by letting them ask questions via email.

Remember follow up doesn't end if they join the team. You'll need to mentor them and provide proper training so that you don't face the issue of someone coming on board – and then not doing anything.

Chapter 7: Converting Prospects into Distributors or Customers

Converting prospects into distributors or customers will depend on the style of your presentation and your ability to tailor your pitch to the situation at hand. Regardless of what you're trying to sell, establishing a rapport and getting the prospect to reveal their pain points is going to be the path to success. Nobody likes pushy salesmen, and in the case of recruiting prospects to be distributors, that is truer than ever. Tread with caution and use a low-key approach.

Spend time getting to know your pitch

Practice makes perfect in every endeavor in life. Don't go out in the field unprepared and expect to make conversions. Begin by outlining your pitch and then fill it in, and study it carefully. Your pitch should be converted to memory so that it doesn't seem rehearsed or come across as stiff and plastic. Remember your life literally depends on your pitch – so you need to know it inside and out and be able to deliver it flawlessly. Sincerity is a key virtue to have in this business, remember that people are on the lookout for "snake oil salesmen" and getting duped.

You need to have more than one pitch. People are going to be coming to you with their own situations – and the key to closing a sale is solving their problems. While you won't know the specific details of each prospect, you'll find that their problems all fit within a set of narrowly defined areas.

For example, if the prospect is someone that you're trying to recruit to be a distributor, many people are going to have trouble paying their bills. The details of this problem are not that important, what's important is that you can help them solve this problem by offering them an opportunity to make extra money, and maybe more money than they're making at the current job. Others are seeking a life of freedom, escaping the 9-to-5 rat race, or getting away from a nasty boss.

Begin by making a list of problems that people can solve by getting a second income from an at home business that is flexible. Then develop a pitch to address each problem.

Sincerity when delivering your pitch is going to be very important. People aren't interested in making deals with phony salesmen. In fact, for many people, the word "salesman" is a four-letter word – based on their experiences with high-pressure sales types that try to milk people for every last dime.

Something you need to remember about the network marketing industry is that your primary motivation should be to help people and be a leader. Money is a secondary reward that is provided in proportion to the service to humanity that you provide – so don't focus on the money. That doesn't mean you can't be excited about earning a high income; we all would be. The point is you need to focus on the benefits that you're providing people first. When you do that financial reward follows practically in an automatic fashion. If you're sincere and trustworthy, you're going to close with a prospect before your competitors do every single time.

One way to help yourself with these exercises is to put yourself in the shoes of the prospect and see the world through their eyes. As a distributor, you should remember that you were once in their position. That should make it easier to craft a recruiting pitch that doesn't come across as high pressure.

When it comes to selling product, you need to know your pitch as well. You will achieve more success if you are able to position yourself as an authority figure in the particular niche that you're promoting. This will entail a great deal of study. In truth, you're going to be following the same type of program here that you will be following when recruiting new distributors. The first task in crafting a pitch that you can use to sell your products is to know what problems people are having that the product solves. You shouldn't just have a list of what the problems are, but you should study them in depth. Having in-depth knowledge that will confirm what people already know not only establishes you as an authority figure, it will help build trust with prospects.

Once you've identified the problems that are solved by your product, begin crafting your pitch by noting exactly how the product solves the problem. Your presentation shouldn't be robotic, but it should flow seamlessly as if you're just engaged in natural conversation.

Time spent getting to know your pitch will help it come across as completely natural and sincere. Practice your pitch repeatedly and commit it absolutely and totally to memory.

Initiate the conversation with a question

One of the best ways to weave your pitch into a conversation is to ask a question. The question should be directed at revealing a problem the prospect is having. This opening will allow you to inject your pitch into a conversation in a natural fashion. Asking a question opens the door and lets the prospect tell you the problems that they are having. Then you can gently step in and show them that you have thought about the problem and you can help them solve it. Never use high-pressure techniques, which is the worst approach you can use in sales or recruitment. I am reminded of a time that I went to buy a car and was just browsing the lot. At the time I was just in the beginning stages of looking for a car, but an aggressive salesman literally ran after me as I tried to escape. I can assure you I did not return to that dealer's lot.

When you are hosting a group event, asking questions is an excellent technique you can use to flow into your sales pitch. Consider any group of people with a common overarching problem. While there might be many different specific problems in the audience, one thing that is guaranteed is that at least one person – and more likely several – are going to share a common problem. And guess what – you can prepare for this ahead of time and make it the topic of your presentation by simply asking the audience a question.

For example, if you are selling a diet product, your event is obviously going to be attended by people who are overweight and sedentary. Many of them are either going to be diagnosed by their doctor as type 2 diabetics or as suffering from "pre-diabetes." You could ask the audience who among them is dealing with high blood sugars. With a diet product, you're certainly going to find one person –probably several who have this problem. If you get multiple people responding to the question and indicating they have the problem, you immediately create camaraderie among people in attendance. This establishes a baseline for social proof. Once one person with this problem accepts your solution, then others will find it easier to follow.

Answer questions your prospect might have

Whether you are recruiting or selling a product, one of the best techniques is to get the prospect actively involved in closing their own sale. Encourage them to speak up and ask questions. Actively involved prospects are going to feel as though their concerns are being taken into account, and that they aren't being duped by a slick sales pitch.

Make your pitch

In the end, it's time to make your pitch. The overview of the process is:

- Establish trust and rapport with the prospects.
- Present yourself in a friendly and upbeat manner.

- Be enthusiastic, but do it in a reasonable fashion. Don't come across as someone who belongs to a cult.
- Once trust is established, direct the conversation so that prospects reveal their pain points to you.
- Assuming that you've prepared ahead of time, you will have a pitch that has been crafted to address any problem that is going to come up.
- Present your pitch, but make it interactive.
- Bring prospects along by encouraging them to ask questions, and show them that you're inclusive and supportive.

Chapter 8: Creating a Strong Follow-up System

A follow-up system is going to be vital to building your business. Just like in the last chapter, you'll need a follow-up system with your prospects regardless of type. In other words, this includes both people interested in your product as well as distributor recruits. Not all people are ready to buy at first contact; in fact, often times, most people are not ready to buy immediately. So you have to put some effort into preselling and warming the prospect for later conversions.

When to use automated follow-ups

One of the benefits of our modern world is the ability to employ technology in the service of the business. The email has been around in widespread public use for a couple of decades, but despite the explosive growth in technology is remains a mainstay of communication. Email auto-responders are great sales tools and are easy to use. You can set up a low-cost email auto-responder at many companies, such as:

- Get Response
- Aweber
- MailChimp

- Constant Contact

Check out multiple email auto-responders and find one that best fits your business and pricing needs. The most modern auto-responders also include the ability to send text messages – which can be a helpful way to keep you in the minds of your prospects, provided it is done the right way. One service that is highly recommended is called ClickFunnels; it allows you to build drag & drop lead pages for your websites and easily incorporate email auto-responders and automated text messages.

You can have prospects join your email lists by signing up at "landing pages" which are web pages that include a simple email sign-up form. They are very popular with email marketers because they work very well. Once someone opts into your landing page, the email auto-responder kicks into action automatically. You can give clients and prospects a link to your landing page where they can sign up on their own, or you can collect email addresses from prospects you meet in person and manually add them to your lists.

A prospect is warmest at the beginning, but you still don't want to hard sell. Send friendly and informative emails that add value without asking for a sale. You can provide your contact information at the end of each email while encouraging prospects to ask questions, along with links to your sales pages if you are trying to move product.

Landing pages and email auto-responders are very effective tools to use with online promotion on social media and with online advertising. Prospects are very used to this setup, so you're not going to have to explain it to anyone. You can tie a Facebook page to your Facebook ad which goes to the landing page, helping you show the user that you have an established online presence which will help you build trust.

In many cases, it helps to give away a freebie of some kind in exchange for the prospects email address. You can write a small booklet explaining your products if you are using this technique to find buyers for the products. If you are trying to recruit distributors, then you can use an eBook written about the company explaining the benefits of becoming a distributor. It doesn't matter who your target is – be sure to include your contact information inside the eBook including your phone number, email address, Facebook page, and other information.

The landing page will become a central part of your automated follow-up system. You should link to it any chance you get, from your YouTube videos, blog posts, and your Facebook page.

Automated responders can also be used to set up webinars – this is a very effective marketing technique. You can use webinars in every aspect of your business, so you follow the same procedure outlined above, adding people to your email list while giving away some sort of free gift, and then you register them for a webinar. In general, webinars should be used for selling big-ticket items, but you can use them to sell anything from about $195 up depending on the level of attendance. Webinars are a great way to recruit new distributors.

Your automated responder, regardless of the end goal, should send a welcome email immediately when someone signs up and opts into the email list. Often people call email autoresponders "newsletters" in order to make them seem less threatening and intrusive to prospects.

After this, you should stagger your emails, gradually widening the time in between emails. Send the second email about two days later, and add one day in between each send. Your warmest prospects are going to convert sooner rather than later, and putting much effort into chasing down the one remaining prospect that might convert isn't the best use of energy, but the beauty of this setup is that it's automatic, so the only effort you have to put in is once – at the front end. That is when you write your emails. After the first month, you might want to drop off the frequency to once a month out to about one year in total.

You will want to use your emails to develop trust with your prospects. You want to get them to see you as an authority figure, so be sure to dispense useful, free advice in your emails. In the beginning, put a mild pitch at the end of each email, but after about 2-3 emails you can occasionally do a hard sell. After a hard sell, send an email which is strictly informative about your niche without doing any selling or product pitch at all. Then gradually repeat the process.

If you are selling multiple products, you can have distinct email lists for each product and pitch them separately. You will also have an email list for prospective distributors. Most services allow you to move a prospect from one email list to another, so after a prospect purchases, you can move them to a separate list that only includes customers that have purchased. Perhaps you can offer them a big ticket item on this list since you know they are warm to purchasing. You can also pitch the idea of becoming a distributor to clients who make product purchases and send them to a landing page that is designed for that purpose so that they can sign up and join your distributor prospects email list.

When you have a prospect's email, it's a potential gold mine since you are in personal contact with them. Use this to the fullest potential.

Text messages should be used sparingly, but if you are going to be having a large upcoming event, such as a product demonstration in person or a webinar, you can use text messages to alert people about it and send them where they need to go for more info. When recruiting distributors, automated text messages can be a useful tool, to prompt people to contact you so they can discuss the program.

Manual follow-ups

Do you like engaging with people directly? Manual follow-ups are a definite tool you should use when following up with prospects. A network or multi-level marking business is based on **networking** with people. This is best done in person. However, before we go on – every MLM marketer these days should have an automated system in place. It will run on autopilot and can be finding warm prospects for you 24/7, often from around the world. In today's world there is no reason to limit yourself to those people that you contact directly, in person, and locally. You may even be able to create a massive network across multiple countries.

That said, manual follow-ups still have their place. Relationship building is a central part of network marketing and doing it on the telephone and in person is still by far the best way to do it. For many people, manually following up can be difficult. The best advice when manually following up is to treat this as if you are contacting a trusted friend. You want to be relaxed, natural, and basically just be yourself.

One thing that helps manual follow-ups operate more smoothly is to use the same process each and every single time. Yes, the specific pitch might be different, but if you follow the same overall process so that it becomes second nature, you can avoid appearing stiff or pushy, two things that while not related will drive prospects away.

The first rule of using manual follow-ups in the modern world is to get your prospects in your automated follow-up stream as a backup. That said, when you can, use a manual follow-up do it.

It's important to avoid letting the prospect get in touch with you, although you should always provide them with contact information in case they want to contact you with questions. However, remember that while your prospects may be on your mind, as the seller, you're generally not going to be the top priority for most people. They are busy with their own lives, and although they may be interested in your products or in becoming a distributor, they are also going to work each day, taking care of the kids, paying bills, and so on. You are probably #5 or #10 on their list. So it's up to you to reach out and make contact at appropriate intervals, rather than sitting back and waiting for the prospect to get in touch with you.

Always be courteous, polite, and professional when trying to follow-up. It's better to follow-up sooner rather than later. Remember that you need to strike when the iron is hot. People may lose interest if too much time goes by. Try to pin a prospect down to a specific time for a phone call or meeting within the next 2-5 days. The sooner, the better, the following day or within 48 hours is far better than five days down the road. Let the prospect select the time for the follow-up so that you demonstrate you are concerned about their needs and that you're entirely flexible.

Avoiding anything that reeks of the hard sell during manual follow-up is critical. You don't want to appear needy. While you may be excited about closing a specific prospect, you have to remember that there are more where they came from. If you come across as desperate or needy, the prospect will be turned off and view you as an annoyance. If you are just getting started and you need to earn money fast, it's going to be tougher to avoid looking needy, but you must do it for your long-term success. Also, be nuanced about persuading someone into a sale, rather than pressuring with a hard sell.

Sometimes people are ready to buy but hesitant, and they want validation for specific concerns. Be on this lookout for this and be ready to mirror their concerns, while providing the solutions that they seek. Every time in marketing you should always be ready to frame a product or service in terms of how it's going to solve the prospect's problems. This will help validate their desire to purchase and get them to move off the fence.

If you are recruiting distributors, one easy way to get into the right mindset is to remember that you're giving them an opportunity. You're offering them a chance to join a team that will help them generate their own at home business income and provide them with more freedom and liberty. So you don't need to hard sell them. The opportunity will sell itself; all you have to do is make sure they are informed as to what the benefits are.

Don't be afraid to use your upline for assistance and coaching. If you have a difficult prospect, you can bring the upline in to help close the deal, whether they participate directly or if you simply get coaching from them. In either case, get yourself in a learning state of mind so that you won't need outside help next time.

One of the ideas I learned from internet marketing is that you have to actually ASK the prospect to close the deal. Online, this is done by giving them a purchase link or button at the right moment. When doing a manual follow-up, you need to do this as well. Don't be afraid to ask the prospect to close on the sale. You don't start out with this – warm them up first.

Timing is critical with follow-up. People will begin losing interest and doubts will creep in. Oftentimes they will start speaking with others, who not really knowing anything will discourage your prospects. If they find out that it is multi-level marketing, they may act on their stereotypes rather than on real information. These are some of the reasons it's important to follow-up quickly.

Don't be hesitant about continuing with a second follow-up meeting or phone call. Use the same techniques you used for the first follow-up. So you pin them down to a specific time while letting them sort out their own schedule. Never looked forced. If they refused to set a second follow-up, then let a day or two go by for a cooling off period and try and contact them again.

Knowing when to stop following up

Be aware of signals that your prospect simply isn't interested. There are several things to look for, and if you've ever dated anyone, you should be looking for the same signals. If you place a call with someone and it keeps going to voicemail, but they never call you back, that might be a signal to back off. Use common sense. You wouldn't call someone 10 times a day to ask them on a date (at least we hope not), apply the same rule when trying to convert prospects. Since this is business and not personal, you should set a rule that you follow where you'll simply leave prospects alone. A good rule is two calls maximum that isn't returned. In order to make sure that the prospect simply isn't missing your attempts to contact them, send them an email as well as your final communication. Let them know that you tried calling them and you're sorry that you weren't able to connect and invite them to contact you if they are still interested. If recruiting distributors, you might ask if they know someone else who would be interested in this money-making opportunity they are choosing to pass by. But be friendly about it and make sure you don't come across as snarky or pushy.

If you've set up an in-person meeting, and the prospect fails to show, this can be disconcerting. The reality is that some people who've lost interest will simply stop contacting you without explanation. It's important to avoid pressuring people, but if they don't show you should try to contract with a combination phone call and email. Sometimes people do forget, or something comes up, and they don't have the time to let you know they aren't showing, so you have to give people a little bit of a benefit of the doubt. But if they don't return your phone call and email, then let that prospect go.

Remember the world is full of prospects – so there is no point wasting energy continually trying to corner one particular prospect. Someone who has lost interest isn't worth wasting your time on when you can move on to a better prospect that will convert.

Chapter 9: Building an Effective Downline

In a network marketing business, an effective downline will make or break your business. Sure, you might be able to slog on making small or even reasonable amounts of money, but if you want to truly grow your business and reach the heights that you dream of, you need to build an effective downline. The first step in this direction is finding appropriate prospects for your downline. You don't want to recruit just anyone. As part of your role in recruiting and building your downline, you're going to want to fill the role of a leader, rather than being a "boss." As a leader part of your role will be to help your downline grow their own businesses and wealth. It's a win-win relationship. A leader will act as a mentor and provide support, not just give direction. As you build your downline, a large part of your role will be training and providing inspiration. As you build your downline, you will grow as much as your team.

Finding prospects for your downline

Leveraging the power of a network marketing business is how you take your own business to the highest peaks it's capable of reaching. That power comes from having a downline, where you have a mutually beneficial relationship. You will help the members of your downline establish their own successful businesses, and in turn personally benefit financially from their own growth. This is why the network marketing model is such a powerful way to build a sales force. Everyone wins, and they all manage their own independent businesses and yet are part of a larger team and a business.

When finding prospects for your downline, remember that you are offering them an opportunity. So you should approach your prospects without fear or without worrying about rejection. If they pass on the opportunity, so be it — no point in wasting time, move on to the next prospect.

You can find prospects anywhere you can do business. Finding prospects online is a great way to start, and a way that you can expand well beyond your own hometown. Depending on the company you join, you may be able to recruit overseas. Some companies may not allow this; you will have to check with your specific company to see what they allow or don't allow as far as your expansion and recruitment of your downline. In any case, using online tools will always be beneficial even if you restrict yourself to recruiting locally.

You can also recruit using free advertising on Craigslist. Be careful about how you word your ads, Craigslist can be strict sometimes about what they will or won't allow on their site. Also, some Craigslist users are fanatical zealots who will spend time trying to dig up ads that violate the site's terms and conditions.

When advertising on Craigslist, you won't want to reveal that it's an MLM or work from home business explicitly, but don't be deceptive. You should mention an approximate level of compensation and direct people to email you for more information. When prospects email you, then you can have them directed to a signup landing page, or you can contact them and ask for their phone number and other information to establish direct contact. Craigslist has sales categories in their employment section where you can post these ads. Keep in mind that the site is focused on being local if you want to post to multiple locations change up your ad since they are on the lookout for duplicate ads.

Engaging with your prospective downline

When engaging with your prospective downline, the first rule of the day is to be friendly. Seek out and start building friendships with prospects, and share with them your enthusiasm and excitement about this business. Do it without being pushy, but make sure you communicate what you need to communicate.

As we mentioned earlier, establishing trust is one of the most important techniques used in sales. Recruiting prospects might seem to be a different activity, but when it comes down to it recruiting is nothing more than sales. So you will want to approach your prospective downline in much the same way you'd approach someone you were selling a product to.

Begin by establishing trust, and set yourself up as an authority figure in the industry. Also, make sure your prospects see you as someone they can go to for potential solutions to their problems. Part of this will involve getting them to open up their pain points and problems to you. This can be done by establishing a good rapport.

Once you know someone's pain points, as related to potentially joining the business, then it's a simple matter to sell the business to them. Typical pain points are not being able to pay the bills, being unable to save enough money for the kids' college, going bankrupt, being bored at their current job, wanting to work from home, or wanting to grow rich rather than slog through life in a middle-class lifestyle. Once you find out which specific problem your prospect is dealing with, then you can put forward joining the networking business as the solution to their problems. As you can see from the list above, a network marketing business solves all of them and many other problems.

To be as effective as possible, you should prepare for each possible problem ahead of time, and work out a sales pitch for each. Then you should know the sales pitch inside and out, which means you'll have to devote time to studying your own sales pitches.

Also, go through each sales pitch and work out possible objections, and your answers to them. Remember that people love experts who are sure of themselves without being pushy, so you want to frame yourself as a friendly authority figure who cares about their associates, and it's you and the network marketing business that can help solve their problems.

People who truly need to make extra money will feel like a great weight has been lifted off their shoulders when they know they are joining a successful and supportive team that can help them reach their financial and lifestyle goals. Make sure that you explicitly communicate to them that you're going to do this.

Always be prepared, so have literature and other aids that your company provides to hand out to new prospects. Make sure to use a strong follow-up program as well. Share your enthusiasm and energy – both of which are contagious. Let people know they are going to be joining something big, which will be exciting and help them reach their true financial potential while achieving strong personal growth. People want to experience personal growth in their careers, and network marketing is one of the most effective ways they can do this. Make sure they know this – it's up to you to teach them about it.

While many new MLM members approach friends and family, you should not aggressively pitch people you have personal relationships with. This will simply turn you into an annoyance. You can let people know what you are doing and show with action the benefits – that may be enough to help you recruit friends and relatives. Let them come to a decision on their own.

Being a network marketer requires you to be social and outgoing. Part of this will be learning the art of approaching new prospects and selling them on it. Learn to start conversations with strangers, and weave your business into the conversation while making it look natural. Never look like you're hard selling. You should attend events related to your MLM business niche and look for prospects there – these are people already interested in your niche and potentially excited about promoting it.

Qualifying your downline to find the best team members

Begin building your downline by sorting out the right members. Some questions you need to ask people are they happy? Do they have a plan to improve their future? Chances are the answers to these questions will be No and NO. When people reveal that they don't have a plan, that is when you let them know that you happen to have a plan to help them solve their problems and build a new and better life. However, show people your plan (which is joining your exciting team) without hard selling them. People don't like to be pressured.

Remember that your prospects are going to represent you. So you're going to want to look for prospects that display ethics and integrity. They should have evidence in their background that they are willing to work hard and go the extra mile. Education isn't as important as a willingness to learn. Sales experience isn't required, but of course, it can be helpful. It's more important that people are outgoing and enthusiastic.

Someone's financial status can be something to consider. Some people recommend qualifying prospects that are currently employed because they will have an income they can tap to get their business off the ground. However, sometimes people in a financial pinch might be better prospects because they are going to be highly motivated. You will have to evaluate each prospect on their own and weigh problems they are having against their good points. Everyone is down on their luck at some point in their lives, and maybe you were when you first decided to change things by going into network marketing.

You will definitely want to recruit prospects who have an entrepreneurial mindset. This doesn't mean Thomas Edison or Steve Jobs. You're looking for people willing to strike out on their own. In network marketing, people aren't getting paid to show up to an office. They have to run their own business and generate their own income. Living this way requires that people have an entrepreneurial mindset.

How people treat customers is going to be an important part of your business. You are going to want to seek out people who will not discriminate. It's important to accept customers for who they are including age, race, gender, ethnicity, sexual orientation, religious beliefs, and so on. Anyone who has a problem with treating everyone equally and in a respectful, friendly demeanor doesn't belong on your team.

The communications style should be open and friendly. They should also show enthusiasm, which is important to keep the business growing by selling products and recruiting new members. Remember that while you're recruiting new members, your recruits are going to be doing this as well. The continued growth of the business requires that they be able to do this effectively. You will have to evaluate prospects on their ability to help you with recruiting, not just selling products.

Prospects who are prone to criticizing others or engaging in gossip are not the type of people that you want as a part of your business.

In summary, respect, ethics, hard work, enthusiasm, friendliness, commitment, and joy are the characteristics to look for to build a successful team.

The importance of service-based leadership

In any business, service is the ultimate key to success. This is very important for a multi-level marketing business. You earn money by providing service. Money is nothing more than a medium of exchange, but the more service you provide others, the more they will be willing to pay you. Service for retail customers will result in more direct sales. Each person will be paid in proportion to the amount of service that they provide. That is why a brain surgeon is paid more than a janitor.

As a leader of your team, you will gain much by providing service to your team. The more service you provide, the more they will work hard to make sales helping everyone earn commissions. You'll provide service by properly training your downline so they can do their jobs to the fullest extent possible. You will provide service by setting everyone up for excellence. When you set up mutually beneficial relationships in this manner, your downline will return the favor ten-fold.

Service also means providing support. Your downline should be comfortable coming to you with problems or asking for support. You should be ready to help your downline close product sales or recruit new members. The relationship between a leader and their downline should be a win-win relationship.

Be a leader, not a boss

We've all had bosses. Bosses are controlling and thrive on giving orders. Employees are not the equal of their boss. A leader, on the other hand, wants their downline to excel as much as possible. It's a mutually beneficial relationship rather than a master-servant relationship the way a boss-employee relationship is structured. You are part of a team, and in a structure that is more akin to a football team as an example. The quarterback is the leader of the team, but he is not the boss. Every player is an integral part of the team, and it can fail if any single one of them fails.

A network marketing organization is very different from the standard type of business, where there is a boss that acts as an authority figure. In a network marketing business, while people in the upline can be viewed as leaders and authority figures, their authority isn't absolute because downline members are growing and expanding on their own and acting as independent entities. Downline members are going to become leaders in their own right. As such a networking marketing business has a duality associated with it that a regular business does not have.

Learn how to manage your time

While team building and recruiting are important, you need to manage your time effectively. Remember that ultimately the company exists to sell products. Make sure that you're devoting adequate amounts of time to all aspects of the business.

Stay consistent in your leadership

A good leader is someone who can be counted on in a crisis and who is consistent. People in the downline will not be happy with a leader who demonstrates and inconsistent leadership style. It makes expectations unclear and drives the entire business into a zone where everything seems arbitrary. This can make people unhappy, and you might find some of them leave.

Keep the lines of communication open

A good leader is always available. You need to provide support to your downline when they need it and be available to answer any questions and provide guidance.

Encourage your downline to leverage their strengths

Every member will be unique, but by building a team, you create a winning group that utilizes everyone's strength in the pursuit of overall goals. As a leader of the team, it's up to you to bring out the best qualities in your team and get people to focus on their strengths.

Train, inspire, and motivate

A leader is someone who inspires and motivates. You will do this in part by setting an example. Don't just talk, show your downline how to conduct business effectively. Demonstrate respect, ethics, and fairness through action. You will also want to be an effective speaker who can motivate the team to perform at their best level. Training is an important part of developing an effective team. You need to make sure that your members have adequate training so that they know all about the products in your line and how to sell them. They will also need their own leadership training, and you'll need to teach them how to recruit their own downline.

Chapter 10: Social Media Marketing

Social media has become the go-to online solution for business. It makes it possible to leverage the natural interconnectivity of people that makes spreading messages super effective. You can incorporate social media marketing into your networking business using both free and paid approaches. Social media is very powerful. It will allow you to reach more people than ever before possible. Network marketers from ages past would look at social media with complete wonder, and they would be justified in doing so. There are many channels and strategies you can use in social media marketing, and you should interconnect them to leverage the power of social media to the fullest. The anchor for your social media efforts should be a blog where you post quality content. Returning to our section on branding, you will want to focus your blog on building your brand either for the product and niche you are involved with or as a tool to sell the business itself and recruit new members. The best approach will be to have two separate blogs for this purpose, but the blog for recruiting new members will probably change at a slower rate than the product blog. Too many network marketers get hyper-focused on recruiting their downline –

remember that first and foremost you are operating a retail business. Blogs develop traffic slowly but when it starts rolling it can really start rolling like a snowball rolling downhill. You will want to post articles about your niche and products on a daily basis, and as we'll see your posts need to be interconnected with your social media accounts. You can post on your recruiting blog once or twice per week and use direct promotion to help people find the blog. Both blogs should be cross-linked with each other.

Setting up a website and blog

While it seems passé, a traditional website and blog will be the core of your business. An online presence can help drive higher levels of sales, often from prospects that you'll never meet in person. There are many alternatives available for setting up online stores and blogs, including Wix, Weebly, and Shopify. Blogs can often be integrated into these online shops directly. Your blog should tie directly with the shop, discussing the niche and specific products in your line.

You should also set up a separate blog and website for your recruiting efforts. That site and blog can be relatively static. Post articles that explain the opportunity and how to contact you if people are interested. You can cross-link between your recruiting blog and the main product blog so that people who are interested in the products who may be open to joining your network marketing organization can read about it. Also, you want to capture prospects that come across your recruiting blog that might be interested in buying and trying out the products.

Your blog will be the focal point of your online presence, and you will link back to it from your presence on social media and vice versa. The blog will form the backbone of comment on your Facebook page, but of course, it does not have to be the only source of content for the Facebook page.

Facebook

Over the past decade, Facebook has taken the world by storm, and with good reason. Facebook provides an unprecedented opportunity for you to promote your networking marketing business. The first step in doing this is to visit Facebook business to create a business identity for yourself – if you want to. The first thing to note is that a small business can't just go and create a Facebook account; you have to use your personal account to start. That said, you can create Facebook pages that are publicly distinct and separate from your personal Facebook account. How you set this up is up to you, and some network marketers prefer to tie everything together publicly. You can invite friends and family to like your network marketing Facebook page to help generate some early publicity, but remember that when someone likes your Facebook page, they will see everything you post on it show up on their timeline. For this reason, some network marketers prefer to keep things separate so that their personal friends and family don't feel like they are shoving the network marketing business down their throat. This is something you will have to decide for your own personal situation.

Before you create your Facebook page, you should post 10-20 articles on your product/niche blog that are rich in content. The content doesn't have to be entirely your own, and easy way to start getting content on a blog is to embed relevant YouTube videos on the blog and write your own commentary below the video. Being original is important; however, even if you are commenting on a video made by someone else. Another good source of content is to post book reviews for related books on Amazon that either promote your niche or working in network marketing itself. Top 10 lists are a good way to add original content and also rise up in search engines.

After you have created your blog articles, begin dripping them onto your Facebook page. Put about 2-3 per day – on your Facebook page, put a short comment that describes what the blog post is about and then add a link to the blog article. It's good to have images at the top of each blog article, Facebook looks for them and shows them on the Facebook page in the post.

The backlinks to your blog will help improve the standing of your blog articles in search engines.

You can also post products in your Shopify or other stores on your Facebook page, to help drive traffic to your online sales presence. Do this sparingly, and you want to use the blog and Facebook page to build a friendly rapport with your customers rather than pushing sales at them aggressively. A reasonable rule to follow is 3-4 posts of CONTENT followed by one post promoting a product. Often an excuse to post a product is a good reason to put one up – such as offering a coupon or special discount if you are able to offer them.

The true power of Facebook is to expand your audience using advertising. You can run periodic advertising campaigns that are relatively inexpensive. The ads can go to your Facebook page (a "likes" campaign), to your blog, or to your online store. You will want to run all three types of campaigns and possibly some others as well. A likes campaign can be very effective, remember that when people like your page then they'll see your future posts on their timeline, and many will share relevant posts with friends bringing more customers.

What really generates power in Facebook advertising is being able to laser target your prospects. You can do this in multiple ways, such as targeting by location, gender, and age. So if you wanted to advertise your skin care products to women aged 35-54 living in Dallas, you could do that. Or you could target a different product to women 65+ living in Florida. The possibilities are literally endless.

You can also target people who have expressed interest in network marketing so Facebook ads can be used as a downline recruiting tool. As discussed previously, you should set up so-called "lead" or "landing" pages. These are simple one-page websites that offer a "free gift" in exchange for the visitor providing contact information. Your free gift can be anything including a physical product, but digital products such as a book or guide in PDF format about your niche are quite acceptable and commonly given. However, if you can afford to do it a free physical product (with the prospect paying for shipping) can also be an effective way to draw in prospects.

The key is to collect the email address so that you can put the person in your automated sales funnel.

So, you will create a Facebook ad with a video. You can create a video to showcase a product or have a short video that simply promotes it. If you are recruiting for the downline, you can use videos where you talk to the camera describing your operation, or maybe your company even has videos and images you can use in Facebook ads for this purpose.

Be careful in the way you describe the business. Facebook may have unfair policies regarding network marketing or MLM businesses. For example, they don't allow you to advertise "work from home" opportunities so you will have to be clever in how you present it so that prospects get the message, but the Facebook censors don't get triggered.

YouTube

YouTube is one of the most powerful social media platforms around. People are visual, and so, they automatically get drawn to video. Your videos don't have to be fancy, simply set up a clean place to shoot. You can even use a smartphone to shoot the video – professional presentations are not required. In fact, an amateurish video seems more real which is why so many YouTubers build up huge audiences of fans with simple videos.

Below your YouTube video, you should include a link to your online store, to your blog, and to your Facebook page. You can also embed links directly in your video. Don't be shy about asking prospects to close the sale – they need the call to action.

It doesn't end there; you want to build a link circle with every presence you have online. This will help pull you up among the search engines. So after posting a video, create a blog post based on the video and link back to your YouTube page from the blog. Then do the same on your Facebook page and any other social media presence you have.

For the network marketer, YouTube should play a central role. You can live stream, demonstrate products, and recruit new distributors using YouTube videos. Moreover, you can use your YouTube videos as advertisements on YouTube, appearing on other channels. This will let you laser target prospects in much the same way that you laser target people on Facebook. You can even target specific videos and channels where your ads are going to be shown. So if you have a skincare product you're pitching, you can advertise it on other videos discussing skin care products. Advertising on YouTube is very inexpensive as well; you can get thousands of video views for a few dollars. If you are going to use YouTube, you should enroll in a course that teaches you how to get your keywords, titles, and everything correct so that your videos don't languish in obscurity. Udemy is a good place to look for courses.

Instagram

Instagram is another very popular social media network. You can promote primarily using images on Instagram, but you can also post "stories" which are short vertical videos. Search online for a marketing tool which is designed to create professional story videos, and then you can post them on your Instagram account. However, the best way to leverage Instagram is to make deals for people to post your material on their account. Instagram users that have large numbers of followers are willing to post other people's material for a fixed amount of time for small fees. Make sure that anyone you approach for such a deal has at a minimum 50,000 followers, and that they will post a link back to your shop, sales page, blog, or YouTube video. Typically an advertised post like this will be up for 12-24 hours. These are independent deals you make directly with the popular person who has the Instagram account. You can probably find deals for $35 or so, but prices may vary considerably depending on the individual you are dealing with. You can also find professional marketing agencies that will help you get promotion through "social influencers" if you prefer that approach, that can help you get a post on Facebook, Twitter, and Instagram simultaneously.

You can also advertise on Instagram, but this is done through Facebook. So, create a Facebook ad if you want to advertise on Instagram. Keep in mind that Instagram has a younger audience, so whether or not you will use them may depend on part on who your prospects are. Ages 18-29 are going to be the dominant age group on Instagram, but that isn't to say there aren't others from different age groups as well.

LinkedIn

LinkedIn can be a very effective platform for recruiting new members for your downline. You can run a blog or advertise on Linked in and target people appropriately. As with other social media platforms, you can backlink to other parts of your online presence. However, LinkedIn will be the most useful when you are recruiting new distributors, not for advertising your products.

Twitter

Twitter can also be a part of your overall online strategy. It's not a platform that you can depend entirely on. While you could rely completely on Facebook or YouTube, Twitter will serve a different, more supportive role. You can use it to help boost blog posts and videos. You can use Twitter to pitch both your products and niche as well as recruiting new members. Twitter posts should always link back to your main website or blog, or the YouTube video you are trying to promote. Posting on Twitter is a good and easy thing to do, but it's not recommended at this time that you spend money on Twitter advertising. That may change in the future.

Pinterest

This is another sharing site that is sort of like Instagram, in that it's a place where you can post images and link back to your sites. Instagram is mobile-oriented, but Pinterest is older and more internet oriented.

Search advertising

Search advertising can be a big part of your online presence. This will work especially well with getting prospects that are in the mind to buy right now. You will need to do keyword research for your niche because search advertising is based on keywords. You need to be ready when you do this, so test and optimize the page you are going to point to with your advertisement before launching a campaign. We say be ready because search advertising can generate large amounts of traffic very quickly, depending on what you use to set your spending parameters and bids. Obviously Google is the go-to network for search advertising; however, you may consider the Bing network, which will run your ads on Bing, Yahoo, and DuckDuckGo. Bing is going to be cheaper than Google Adwords and will still reach a large number of customers. However, if you can afford it be sure to advertise on Google as well.

Chapter 11: Handling Rejection like a Pro

Rejection is an inevitable part of any selling business. In network marketing, you're going to be rejected by clients looking to buy your retail products and then deciding not to, and also by prospective recruits to your team. That means it's going to be more at the forefront than it would be in a regular sales associate type business.

Detach from the outcome

The thing to remember about selling products or recruiting is that any single given sale is not all that crucial. By detaching yourself from the outcome, you can keep an optimistic attitude that will be necessary to close the next prospect that you meet.

Ask why the offer was rejected

Data is king in business, and if you can find out why someone rejected your offer, you can tailor your approach to overcome your weaknesses. However, you need to take a reason given by one prospect with a grain of salt. It may be something that is really limited to that one prospect, but if possible, you should document their reasons for future reference. If you see something that comes up more than once, then retool your pitch.

Don't invest your emotions

Remember tomorrow is another day, and there is always another prospect around the corner. Also, remember that a rejection is not personally directed at you. It's all business and people may very well have their own reasons for rejecting an offer that has nothing to do with you. It's just business – remember this – so don't get emotionally involved with specific sales.

Handle rejection well

Rejection should be handled with poise, grace, and integrity. You should never react angrily toward anyone who rejects your offer. Remember that a prospect that rejects your offer is still a prospect. People often change their minds later – so don't burn any bridges. You want your prospect to remember you as someone who is friendly and respectful and offering opportunity. That way when they reconsider, you will be the first person that comes to mind.

Respect yourself

Rejection can take a toll on people, but remember, it's not personal. Respect yourself and keep an optimistic attitude so that you can dust yourself off and be ready for the next prospect. Prospects are like city buses – there is always another one coming.

Chapter 12: Why Don't Some People Make Money?

Although we'd like to believe that a "system" can be put in place to make sure everyone makes money, this simply isn't true. There are many reasons why that doesn't happen, and we will touch on them in this chapter. Network marketing puts a proven system together that if followed carefully combined with your own efforts will produce results. But it often doesn't work.

Lack of focus and persistence

Focus is an important part of any business. You would be surprised how many people have trouble with focus. Persistence is also a related and important trait that is important for success. Persistence can be the difference between success and failure. Very few people wake up one day as millionaires; most will experience some failures along the way. Those who are persistent work through failures and improve. Those who do not give up and move on without making money.

Focus is important in carrying through to the close. You have to focus on every stage of the business and your development. In the beginning, when you are training, you will need focus. You'll have to focus when you dedicate yourself to learning your niche. Focus will be required when building an online presence if you chose to go that route. Focus will be required to close prospects. At every step of the way, focus plays a central role.

Not learning how to market properly

To reach success, you need to learn how to market properly. If you don't know how, then you need to go to Amazon and buy some books on marketing – and also on sales and copywriting. Learn from the pros who went before you so that you can market properly. If you can't market, then you're not going to make money. There are also plenty of low-cost courses on Udemy and other sites that can help you get started.

Failure to position yourself as a leader

Remember that your business has two foundations – product sales and recruitment. To be totally successful, you'll need to be good at recruitment, and you'll need to position yourself as a leader to get the most out of your downline. If you can't do this, then you can count on the money you make being minimal.

Failure to target your niche

You need to know who your ideal customer is. One good way to do this is to run some Facebook ads showing your products. Do this without any prior targeting. That way, Facebook will tell you, through the results of who responded to your ad, who the typical person is in your niche. This will help you market to the right people. You also need to find out where people in your niche gather. Are there trade shows coming to your city? Do they have clubs and other organizations? You need to find out when and where your niche gathers and take advantage of it.

Making things too complicated

Network marketing is actually quite simple. But many people make it too complicated and get lost in the forest for the trees. This inhibits their ability to be effective and make money.

Getting impatient

Network marketing can lead to tremendous incomes, from a helpful few thousand per month up to six and seven figures. However, it's certainly not a get-rich-quick scheme. The problem is many people view it as a get rich quick scheme, and they also think it is automatic. When they find that they can't make the sales they expected at first when you're learning the ropes, they get impatient and give up. If you come to this with realistic perceptions and realize that building your business takes time, then success will come.

Blaming others

Blaming others will do nothing but create bad karma. Others are not responsible for your failures, and leaders don't blame others. If your downline isn't producing, as a leader you should take responsibility. Don't blame others if your marketing is ineffective and you fail to make sales.

Not wanting to succeed

Your mindset is the most important thing in your foundation. Remember The Secret? This is something that has been taught since Napoleon Hill in the 1930s –you are what you think. Or your thoughts create your reality. Some people don't want to succeed beyond where they are in life – and this desire creates their own reality where they fail in network marketing.

Conclusion

Thanks for taking the time to read this book! If you are completely new to network marketing/multi-level marketing, we hope that it helped clarify what this exciting opportunity is really about. We hope that it will help you decide if you want to join a network marketing organization, how to go about doing it and what to expect.

If you've got some experience, we hope this book helped bring clarity so that you can be even more successful in your network marketing business.

Network marketing provides an unprecedented opportunity for average people to generate wealth, happiness, and independence. It's simply there for the taking. Now, it's up to you to get the right attitude and take what you deserve.

But, remember, there is no free lunch, even with network marketing. Success will depend on your hard work, dedication, persistence, ethics, and enthusiasm. Remember to choose a niche and company that excites you and makes you comfortable – it is only by following a congruent path that you can gain the success that you want.

If you found this book helpful, we would apprieciate an honnest review! We also value any constructive comments about this book.